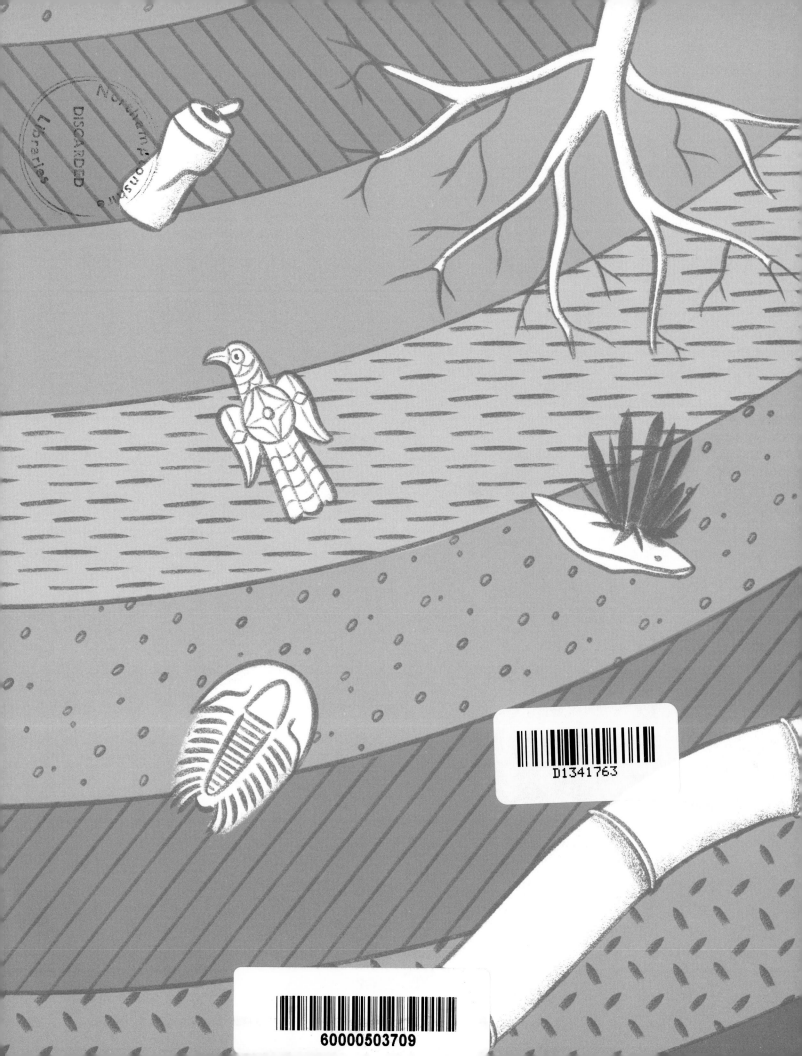

THIS BOOK BELONGS TO

_ _ _ _ _ _ _ _ _ _ _ _ _ _ _

For my family and friends.

This book is dedicated to those who explore the deep,
and especially those working to protect it.

J.M.

*With deep thanks to Dr Catherine Wheller, Hazel Richards, Millie McDonald,
Dr Johanna Simkin, Dr Tom May, Dianne Bray, Caroline Foster and
Alice Sutherland-Hawes for their time and expert knowledge.*

DEEP

JESS McGEACHIN

WELBECK
EDITIONS

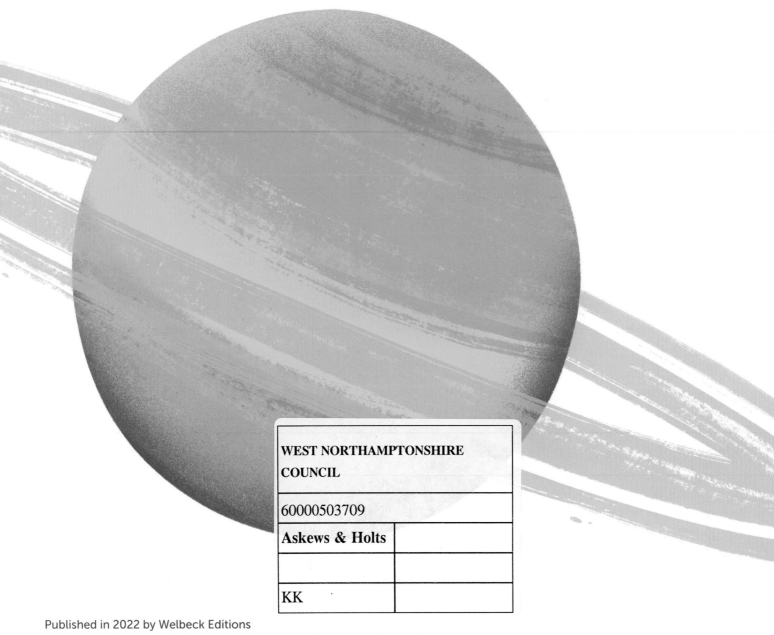

Published in 2022 by Welbeck Editions
An Imprint of Welbeck Children's Limited, part of Welbeck Publishing Group.
20 Mortimer Street London W1T 3JW

Text and illustrations © Jess McGeachin 2022

Associate Publisher: Laura Knowles
Design: Sam James and Jess McGeachin

A CIP catalogue record for this book is available from the British Library

978-1-91351-948-3

Printed in Dongguan, China

10 9 8 7 6 5 4 3 2 1

MIX
Paper from
responsible sources
FSC® C144853
FSC
www.fsc.org

CONTENTS

6 **Welcome to the deep**

8 **Deep Ocean**
10 Giants of the deep
12 It gets weird down here...
14 The ocean floor

16 **Deep Forest**
18 By day, by night
20 One in a million
22 The ground crew

24 **Deep Earth**
26 Hidden treasure
28 Caves
30 A home underground
32 The city below
34 In the sewers
36 Buried secrets

38 **Deep Time**
40 Clues to the past
42 What we leave behind
44 The path ahead

46 **Deep Space**
48 What we can see
50 What we can't see
52 Into the unknown

54 **Deep Inside**
56 Under your skin
58 A team of trillions

60 **Deep connections**
61 **Surviving the deep**
62 **Glossary**
63 **Index**

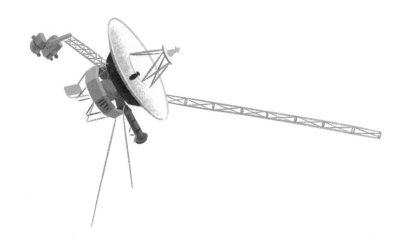

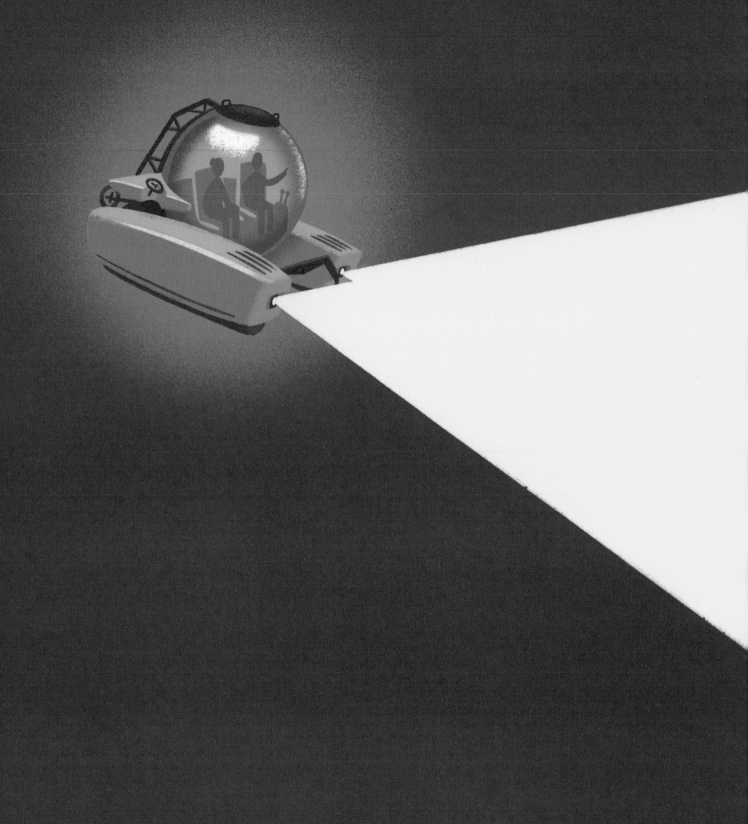

WELCOME TO THE DEEP

Have you ever wondered what lies beyond the edge of our solar system? Or what lives in the cold depths of the ocean, where even sunlight can't reach?

Come on a journey to the deepest parts of our universe — but be warned, things can get a little strange here. Temperatures are extreme, pressure is intense and darkness is everywhere.

Even though these distant places seem far out of reach, what we do still has an impact on them. The lunch you eat affects the trillions of microbes living deep in your gut. The plastics we throw away have been found on the deepest parts of the ocean floor. The clues we find underground can tell stories of those who came before.

We know a little bit about these hidden worlds, but there's much more we don't know. So, what are you waiting for? Dive into the deep...

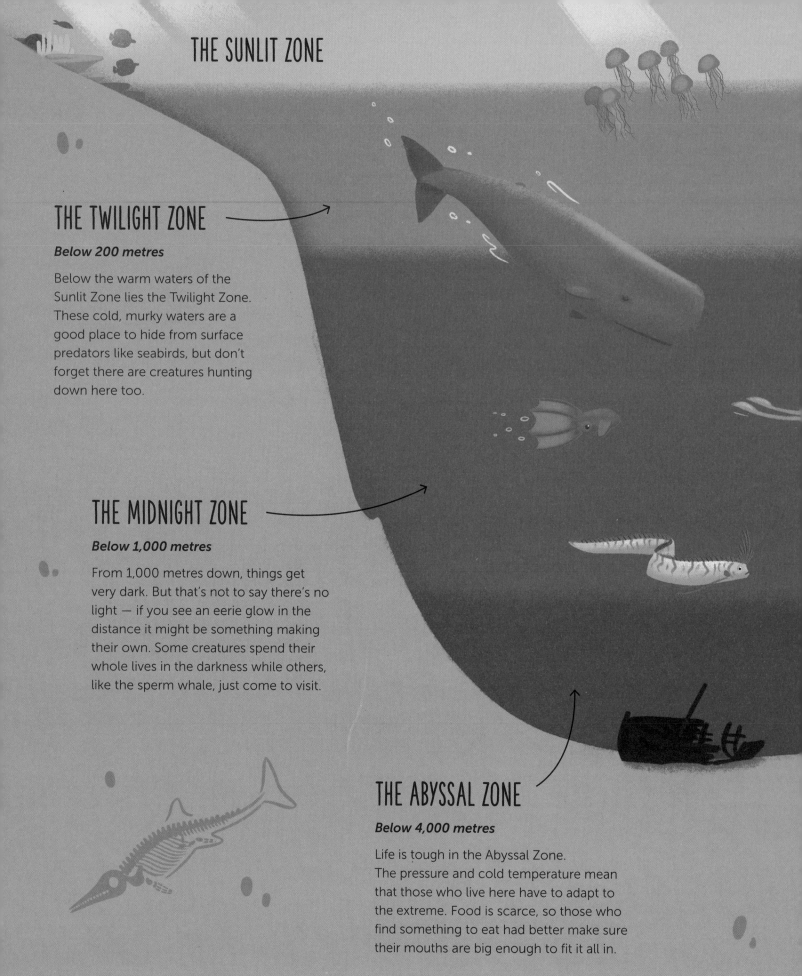

THE SUNLIT ZONE

THE TWILIGHT ZONE

Below 200 metres

Below the warm waters of the Sunlit Zone lies the Twilight Zone. These cold, murky waters are a good place to hide from surface predators like seabirds, but don't forget there are creatures hunting down here too.

THE MIDNIGHT ZONE

Below 1,000 metres

From 1,000 metres down, things get very dark. But that's not to say there's no light — if you see an eerie glow in the distance it might be something making their own. Some creatures spend their whole lives in the darkness while others, like the sperm whale, just come to visit.

THE ABYSSAL ZONE

Below 4,000 metres

Life is tough in the Abyssal Zone. The pressure and cold temperature mean that those who live here have to adapt to the extreme. Food is scarce, so those who find something to eat had better make sure their mouths are big enough to fit it all in.

DEEP OCEAN

Hold your breath and take a journey to the deepest part of our ocean. Don't worry about looking pretty — survival is more important in the deep. Because there's a lot of pressure and very little light, the animals that live here have evolved in unique ways.

THE HADAL ZONE

Below 6,000 metres

What's deeper than the ocean floor? The Trenches. These deep-sea crevasses are home to some of the weirdest creatures of all. Only a handful of people have ever gone this deep and its darkness holds many secrets.

DEEP-SEA CHIMNEYS

When cold seawater leaks through cracks in the ocean floor, it's heated by the molten lava below. As the hot water is released back into the ocean, the minerals it carries create hydrothermal vents. These support a crowded community that includes giant clams and tube worms.

GIANTS OF THE DEEP

It's not your imagination, things really are bigger in the deep. Deep-sea gigantism is a trait that means some animals grow to enormous sizes. It's thought to be a way of adapting to the cold temperatures and lack of food and oxygen. Some, like the giant squid, can grow up to 14 metres in length!

MYTHS AND LEGENDS

Seafarers' tales have inspired countless myths about the 'Kraken' — a huge squid-like creature. Many describe it as a fearsome foe, but in reality the giant squid is no threat to you (unless you're a deep-sea fish).

Oarfish

Snipe eel

VENT YOUR FEELINGS

Giant tube worms

Most living things get their energy from the sun — but not the giant tube worm. These strange animals live on hydrothermal vents in the deep ocean. Bacteria inside them convert chemicals from the vents into food, and in turn they give the bacteria a home.

Giant isopod

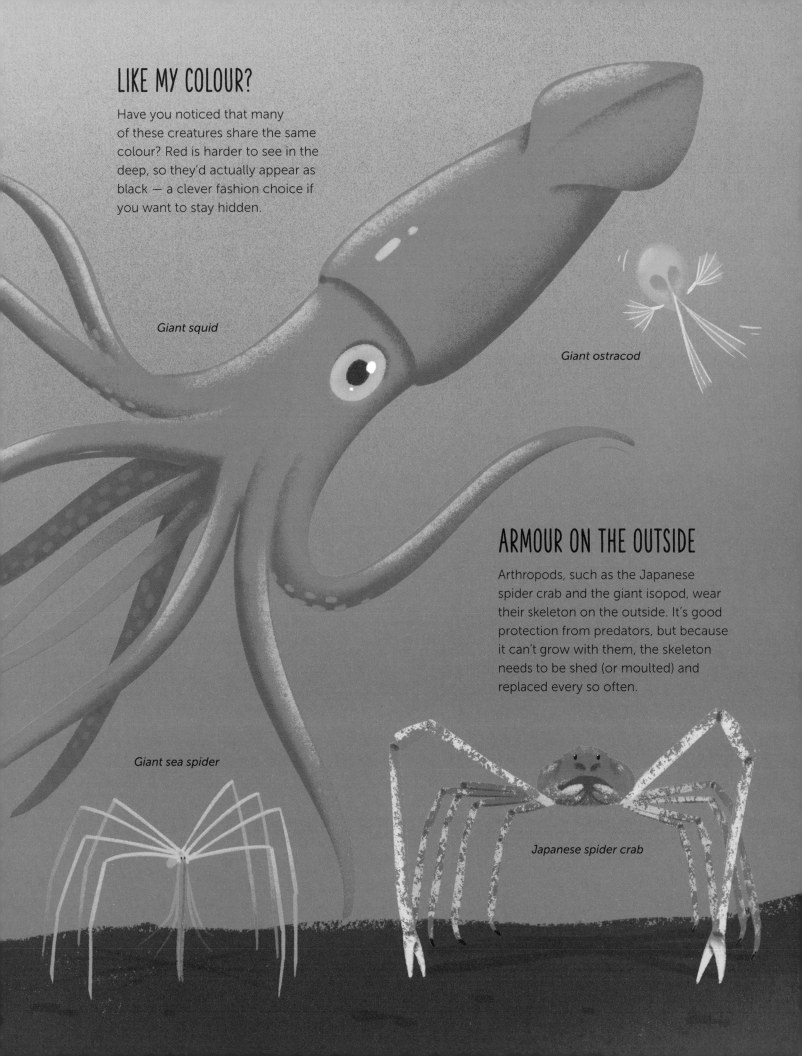

LIKE MY COLOUR?

Have you noticed that many of these creatures share the same colour? Red is harder to see in the deep, so they'd actually appear as black — a clever fashion choice if you want to stay hidden.

Giant squid

Giant ostracod

ARMOUR ON THE OUTSIDE

Arthropods, such as the Japanese spider crab and the giant isopod, wear their skeleton on the outside. It's good protection from predators, but because it can't grow with them, the skeleton needs to be shed (or moulted) and replaced every so often.

Giant sea spider

Japanese spider crab

IT GETS WEIRD DOWN HERE...

The deeper you go, the weirder it gets. Deep-sea creatures have adapted to life in the dark, where their main goal is to eat or avoid being eaten. Don't want to be seen? Try mirrored skin like the hatchetfish. Want to attract some prey? Use your own light like an anglerfish.

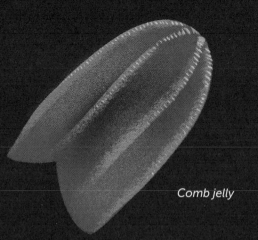

Comb jelly

JUST FINE WITHOUT A SPINE

Animals without a backbone are called invertebrates, and it's a handy quality to have in the deep. Googly-eyed glass squid can enlarge themselves with water, making them look much more intimidating to a predator. They can even use jet-like propulsion for a speedy getaway — whoosh!

Googly-eyed glass squid

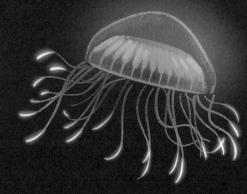

Halitrephes maasi jelly

Jewel squid

HOW LOW CAN YOU GLOW?

Sunlight can't reach the deepest parts of the ocean, so why not make your own? This process is called bioluminescence. Some deep-sea fish use their light as a lure to attract prey, whereas others use it to disguise their shape.

Hatchetfish

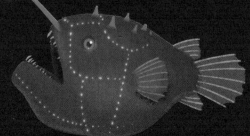

Footballfish

Lanternfish

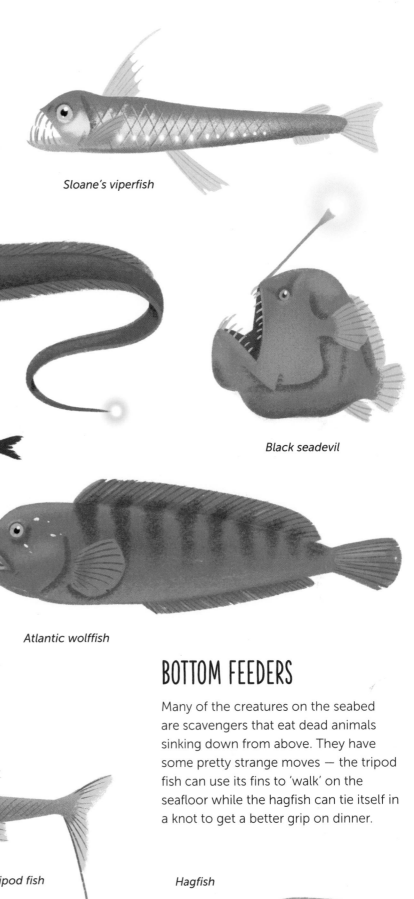

OPEN WIDE

Don't let a small mouth get in the way of a big lunch. Some deep-sea fish have loosely hinged jaws so they can swallow their prey whole. Others have teeth that are so long they can never fully close their mouths.

Sloane's viperfish

Pelican eel

Stoplight loosejaw

Black seadevil

Fangtooth

Atlantic wolffish

BOTTOM FEEDERS

Many of the creatures on the seabed are scavengers that eat dead animals sinking down from above. They have some pretty strange moves — the tripod fish can use its fins to 'walk' on the seafloor while the hagfish can tie itself in a knot to get a better grip on dinner.

Dumbo octopus

Tripod fish

Hagfish

THE OCEAN FLOOR

We've made it to the ocean floor, stretching all the way from the continental shelf down to the abyssal plains and the deep trenches. You might see vast kelp forests or underwater volcanoes but you're guaranteed to find one thing — the impact of humans.

VISITORS FROM ABOVE

Deep-diving submersibles are built to withstand huge amounts of pressure and have taken people all the way down to the trenches. Some even have robotic arms to poke around at the objects they find there.

LOST TREASURES

In centuries past, if you wanted to move your treasure a long way you'd use a ship. And if your ship happened to sink, the treasure might stay hidden. Spanish gold, Roman statues and real pirate loot have all been found on the ocean floor, and if the stories are true, much more remains lost.

SHIPWRECKED

The ocean floor is littered with shipwrecks. Some were tragic accidents while others were intentionally sunk in battle. They can provide clues about their builders, passengers and final journey. Sometimes they also make a wonderful home for the fish!

A LOAD OF RUBBISH

The most common sight down here isn't a fish or crustacean — it's rubbish. Microplastics (tiny fragments from things like plastic bags and bottles) have been found on the seafloor and inside the bodies of deep-sea dwellers. Plastic has even been spotted in the Mariana Trench, the deepest part of the ocean.

THE UNDERSTORY

The lower you go, the darker it gets. The understory is a layer of trees and plants under the canopy where leaves grow bigger to catch the last of the sunlight. As your eyes adjust you might notice snakes twisted around the trees or spy a streak of spotted fur in the distance.

THE FOREST FLOOR

The forest floor is covered in a thick layer of decomposing leaves, fruits and seeds. The nutrients they release are the perfect food for fungi, worms and insects. You might spot a ground-dweller like the white-lipped peccary, whose stomping squadron can break up the soil and help new plants to grow.

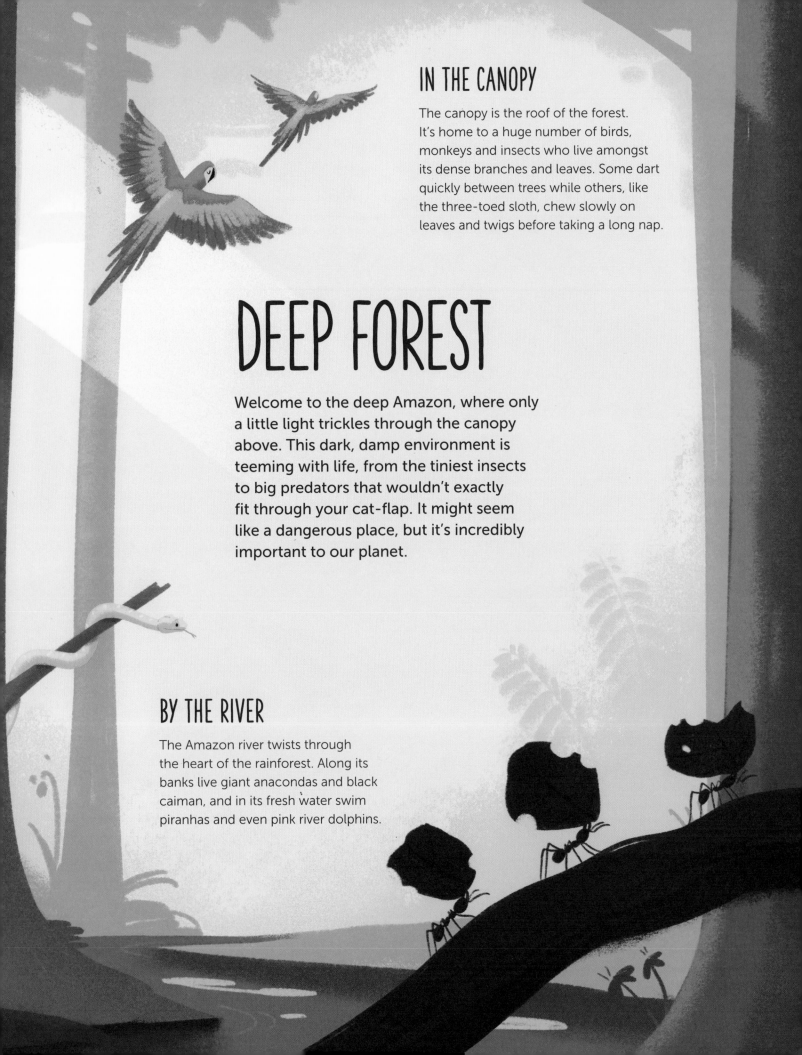

IN THE CANOPY

The canopy is the roof of the forest. It's home to a huge number of birds, monkeys and insects who live amongst its dense branches and leaves. Some dart quickly between trees while others, like the three-toed sloth, chew slowly on leaves and twigs before taking a long nap.

DEEP FOREST

Welcome to the deep Amazon, where only a little light trickles through the canopy above. This dark, damp environment is teeming with life, from the tiniest insects to big predators that wouldn't exactly fit through your cat-flap. It might seem like a dangerous place, but it's incredibly important to our planet.

BY THE RIVER

The Amazon river twists through the heart of the rainforest. Along its banks live giant anacondas and black caiman, and in its fresh water swim piranhas and even pink river dolphins.

BY DAY

If you want to attract attention, the jungle is the place to be. Colourful birds, magnificent monkeys and fluorescent frogs all like to show off — some to find a mate and some as a warning.

Emperor tamarin

Howler monkey

Hoatzin

Amazon kingfisher

MONKEY BUSINESS

The jungle is a noisy place. If you hear a very loud growl it might be a howler monkey, guarding its territory. If you hear a high-pitched whistle it might be a tamarin monkey, calling out to its friends.

BIRDS OF A FEATHER

There are more than 1,500 different types of birds in the Amazon. Some are colourful, some have handy beaks, and some... smell. The hoatzin bird digests its food by slowly fermenting it in its stomach, creating a rather pungent odour. But who wouldn't love that hairstyle?

Poison dart frogs

Tapir

LOOK BUT DON'T TOUCH

There are lots of things you wouldn't want to get too close to in the jungle. Poison dart frogs are beautiful but their bright colours say, 'I'm dangerous, stay away!'. Don't accept a hug from an anaconda; they squeeze a little too tight.

BY NIGHT

Night falls, but don't expect to get much sleep. The loud buzzing of insects rings through the trees and the low growl of a jungle cat reminds you that you're not alone.

Vampire bat

Potoo

WIDE-EYED WONDERS

If you see wide eyes looking back at you from the undergrowth, it might be the nocturnal night monkey or the strange potoo bird. Both have huge eyes designed to see in the pitch darkness of the forest night.

Jaguar

Night monkey

PROWLING PREDATORS

Dawn and dusk are dangerous times in the jungle. Jaguars prowl the banks of the river looking for a tasty meal, but don't think the water is an easy escape — they're excellent swimmers too.

Tarantula

Goliath birdeater

Green anaconda

Giant armadillo

ONE IN A MILLION

If you see a trail of leaves winding through the jungle, it might be an army of leafcutter ants carrying home their spoils. These incredible insects live in sprawling underground nests in colonies of up to 10 million. Each ant has a different job to do, and they grow to different sizes to do it.

Forager ant

CUT AND CARRY

Foragers explore the forest looking for fresh leaves. Once they find the perfect patch they cut the leaves into small pieces using their vibrating jaws and haul them back to the nest. Leafcutter ants can carry loads up to fifty times their body weight!

Gardener Ant

Fungal Garden

FUNGAL FARMERS

Leafcutter ants don't actually eat the leaves they collect. Gardeners chew the leaves and plant them in underground farms where a special type of fungus starts to grow. When it's ready they feed it to the larvae, making them babysitters too.

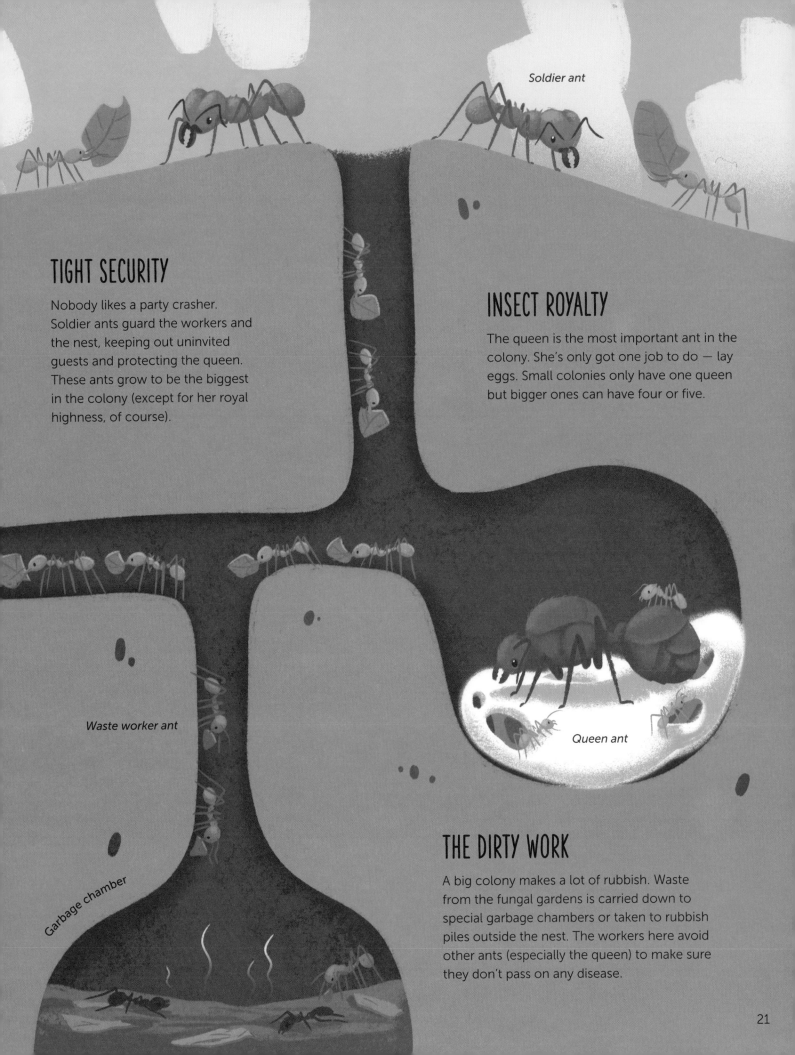

TIGHT SECURITY

Nobody likes a party crasher. Soldier ants guard the workers and the nest, keeping out uninvited guests and protecting the queen. These ants grow to be the biggest in the colony (except for her royal highness, of course).

Soldier ant

INSECT ROYALTY

The queen is the most important ant in the colony. She's only got one job to do — lay eggs. Small colonies only have one queen but bigger ones can have four or five.

Waste worker ant

Queen ant

Garbage chamber

THE DIRTY WORK

A big colony makes a lot of rubbish. Waste from the fungal gardens is carried down to special garbage chambers or taken to rubbish piles outside the nest. The workers here avoid other ants (especially the queen) to make sure they don't pass on any disease.

THE GROUND CREW

The forest floor is teeming with life. This dark, damp place is the perfect home for fungi, who feed on the nutrient rich leaf litter. You might see some of the thousands of insect species that live here too, crawling in the undergrowth. But look closer — some are wearing a disguise!

Basket stinkhorn

Clitocybula azurea

Cookeina sulcipes

FANTASTIC FUNGI

There are thousands of different types of fungi in the rainforest, and each has a different trick up its stem. Stinkhorns emit a terrible smell, earthstar fungi burst into a star shape and *mycena chlorophos* glow in the dark.

Pink oyster mushroom

Bamboo mushroom

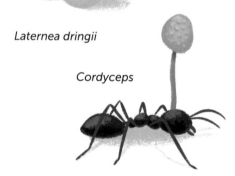

Laternea dringii

Cordyceps

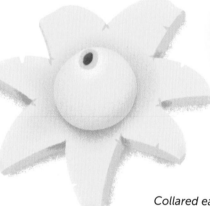

Collared earthstar

Mycena chlorophos

ZOMBIE-MAKERS

Who said zombies aren't real? Some *cordyceps* fungi release spores that can infect ants and control their behaviour. They can make them leave their nest to find a good spot for the fungi to grow. Sadly the ant doesn't survive the process.

Camillea leprieurii

Clavulinopsis fusiformis

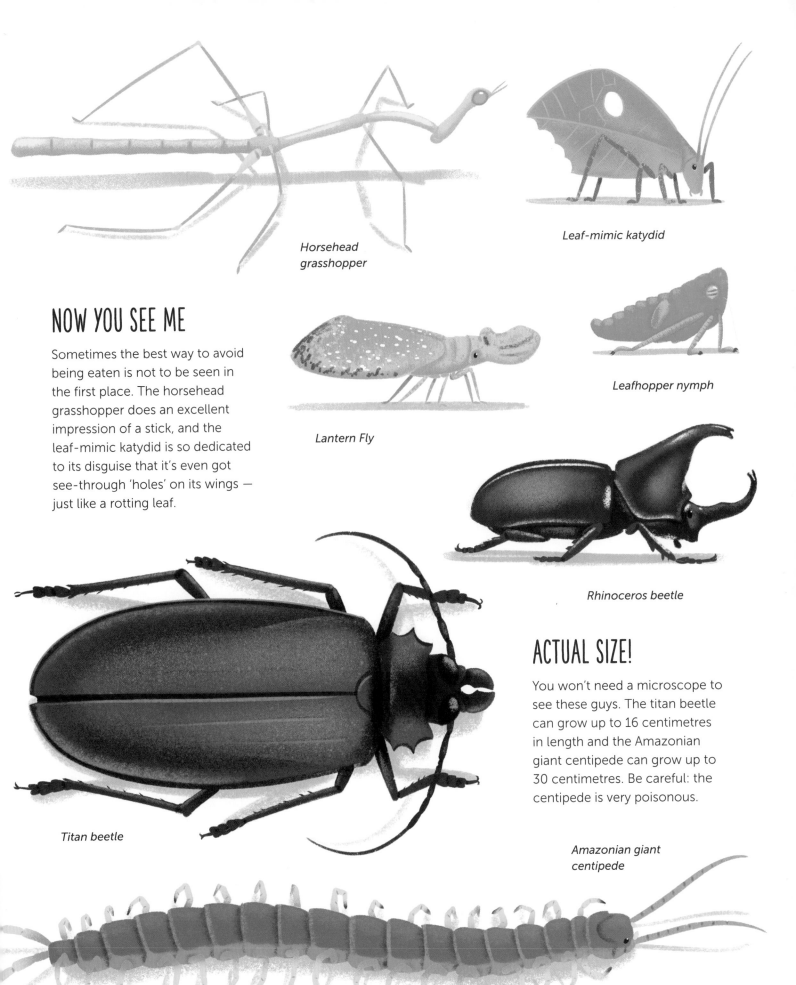

Horsehead grasshopper

Leaf-mimic katydid

Lantern Fly

Leafhopper nymph

NOW YOU SEE ME

Sometimes the best way to avoid being eaten is not to be seen in the first place. The horsehead grasshopper does an excellent impression of a stick, and the leaf-mimic katydid is so dedicated to its disguise that it's even got see-through 'holes' on its wings — just like a rotting leaf.

Rhinoceros beetle

ACTUAL SIZE!

You won't need a microscope to see these guys. The titan beetle can grow up to 16 centimetres in length and the Amazonian giant centipede can grow up to 30 centimetres. Be careful: the centipede is very poisonous.

Titan beetle

Amazonian giant centipede

THE MANTLE

The thickest layer of the Earth is the mantle, a hot and sticky glob of oxygen, magnesium and silicon. Temperatures vary greatly — the upper mantle is cool enough to support the crust, but lower down things start to sizzle as the partially melted rock moves slowly around the Earth.

THE OUTER CORE

Things get a bit more fluid in the outer core. As the Earth spins, currents of liquid iron and nickel flow. This movement creates our planet's magnetic field.

THE INNER CORE

In the centre of our planet sits a scorching hot metal ball, made up of solid iron and nickel. Temperatures reach around 5,400°C here, almost as hot as the surface of the Sun.

THE CRUST

Who said the crust was the boring bit? Along with the upper mantle, the crust forms the hard shell on which we live. It's very thin compared to the other layers, but it keeps the soil and oceans on top and the magma inside (mostly).

DEEP EARTH

If Earth was a cake, it wouldn't be a very good one. The centre is overcooked, the middle is still hot and gooey, and the icing is rock hard with lots of cracks. If it didn't break a tooth it would definitely burn your tongue. As a planet though, it's pretty great. Let's venture below the surface and see what's hiding underneath.

VOLCANOES

Earth gets pimples too. Volcanoes form when magma (molten rock) erupts through the crust. They often occur at the boundary of tectonic plates, where the puzzle pieces that make up the Earth's surface bump into each other or slowly pull apart.

HIDDEN TREASURES

There's a huge amount of heat and pressure under the Earth's surface, two things that are perfect for making rocks and minerals. These come in every shape, colour and size you can imagine and are used for almost as many purposes.

Shale

ROCK ON

When one or more minerals get squished together, it can form a rock. This can happen when lava or magma cools (igneous), when old rocks break apart and are compacted back together (sedimentary) or when heat and pressure change one rock into a new one (metamorphic).

Opal

Pumice

Obsidian

Sulfur

Stibnite

EVERY SHAPE AND SIZE

Minerals are made from different elements. Nearly all minerals form crystals — some as cubes, some as spiky needles and some that are too small to see.

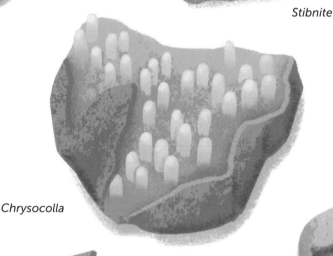

Chrysocolla

Crocoite

Galena

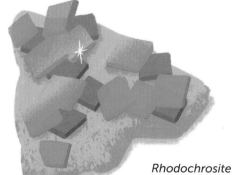

Rhodochrosite

Cyanotrichite

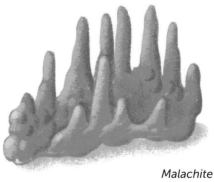

Malachite

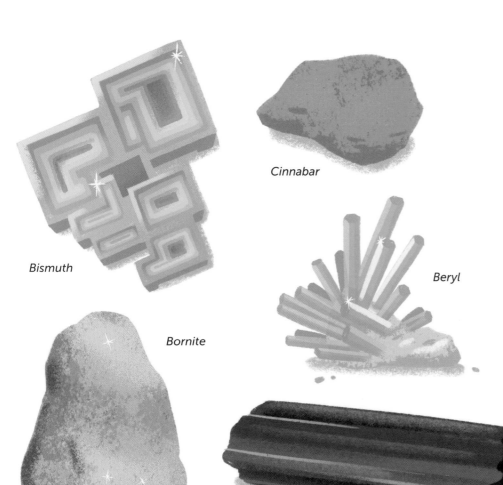

Bismuth

Cinnabar

Beryl

Bornite

PAINT-BY-MINERALS

We've been crushing minerals into pigments for hundreds of thousands of years. Ancient Egyptians used vivid green malachite to paint the walls of their tombs. Bright blue azurite was a favourite of artists in the Middle Ages. Even the fireworks we make today are coloured with different minerals.

Rutile

Azurite

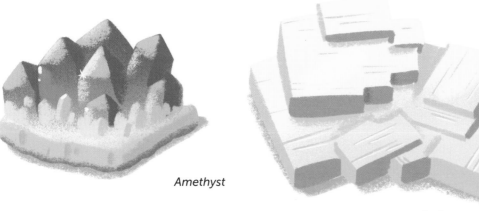

Amethyst

Pyrite

DIGGING UP DANGER

Lots of us benefit from the use of minerals and metals in our phones and computers. But the way we dig them up can cause huge damage to the environment. Mining and greed can unfairly impact local communities and the land on which they, and all of us, rely.

Copper

Hematite

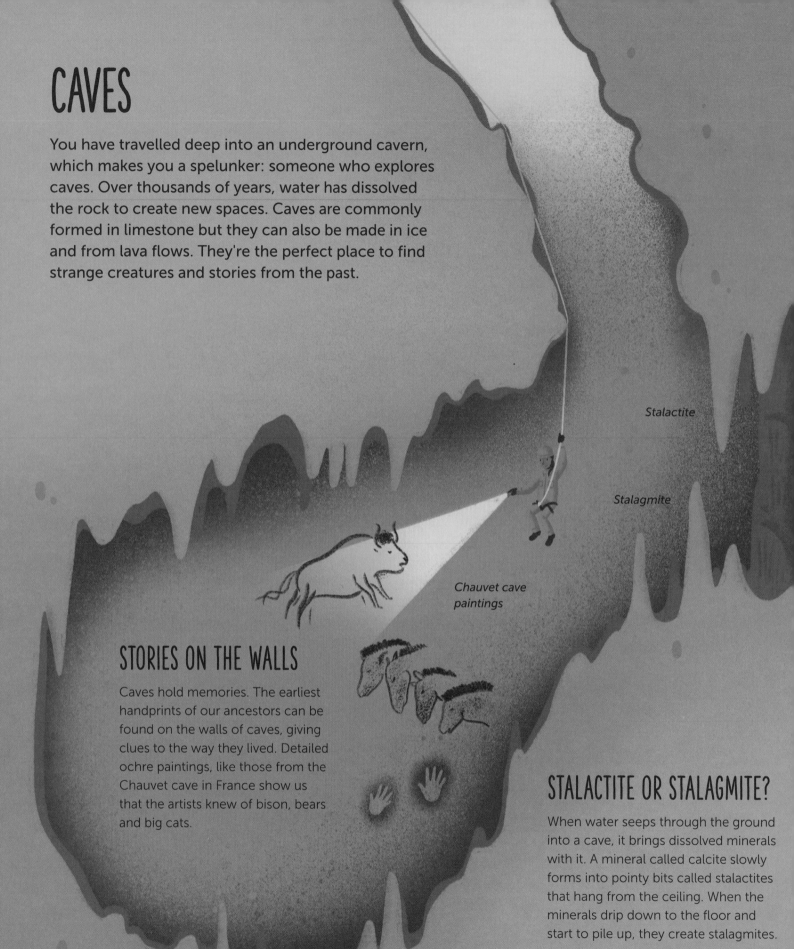

CAVES

You have travelled deep into an underground cavern, which makes you a spelunker: someone who explores caves. Over thousands of years, water has dissolved the rock to create new spaces. Caves are commonly formed in limestone but they can also be made in ice and from lava flows. They're the perfect place to find strange creatures and stories from the past.

Stalactite

Stalagmite

Chauvet cave paintings

STORIES ON THE WALLS

Caves hold memories. The earliest handprints of our ancestors can be found on the walls of caves, giving clues to the way they lived. Detailed ochre paintings, like those from the Chauvet cave in France show us that the artists knew of bison, bears and big cats.

STALACTITE OR STALAGMITE?

When water seeps through the ground into a cave, it brings dissolved minerals with it. A mineral called calcite slowly forms into pointy bits called stalactites that hang from the ceiling. When the minerals drip down to the floor and start to pile up, they create stalagmites.

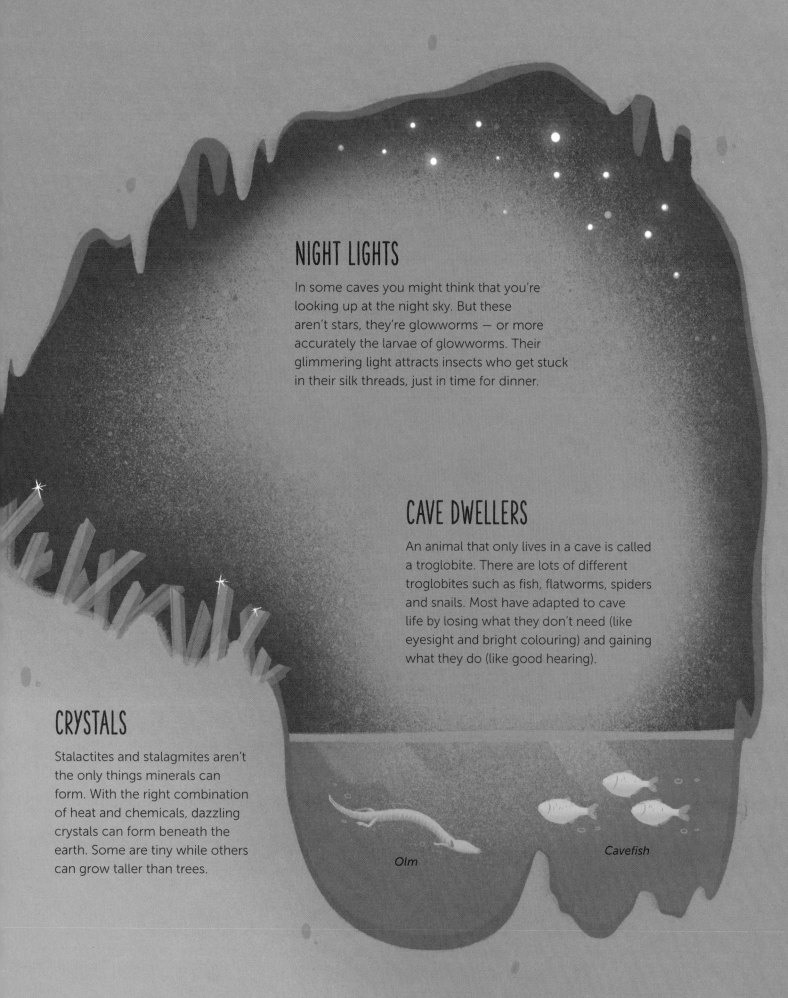

NIGHT LIGHTS

In some caves you might think that you're looking up at the night sky. But these aren't stars, they're glowworms — or more accurately the larvae of glowworms. Their glimmering light attracts insects who get stuck in their silk threads, just in time for dinner.

CAVE DWELLERS

An animal that only lives in a cave is called a troglobite. There are lots of different troglobites such as fish, flatworms, spiders and snails. Most have adapted to cave life by losing what they don't need (like eyesight and bright colouring) and gaining what they do (like good hearing).

CRYSTALS

Stalactites and stalagmites aren't the only things minerals can form. With the right combination of heat and chemicals, dazzling crystals can form beneath the earth. Some are tiny while others can grow taller than trees.

Olm

Cavefish

A HOME UNDERGROUND

If you've ever curled up safe and sound under the blankets, you can imagine what it's like to live in a burrow. These underground dwellings can stay warm in winter, cool in summer, and they're a perfect hideaway from hungry predators above.

Burrowing owl

Rabbit

Mole

Fox

Badgers

SETT FOR WINTER

A badger's burrow is called a sett, and it's the perfect home for a long, cold winter. Like rooms in our houses, badger setts have different chambers for living, sleeping and even going to the bathroom.

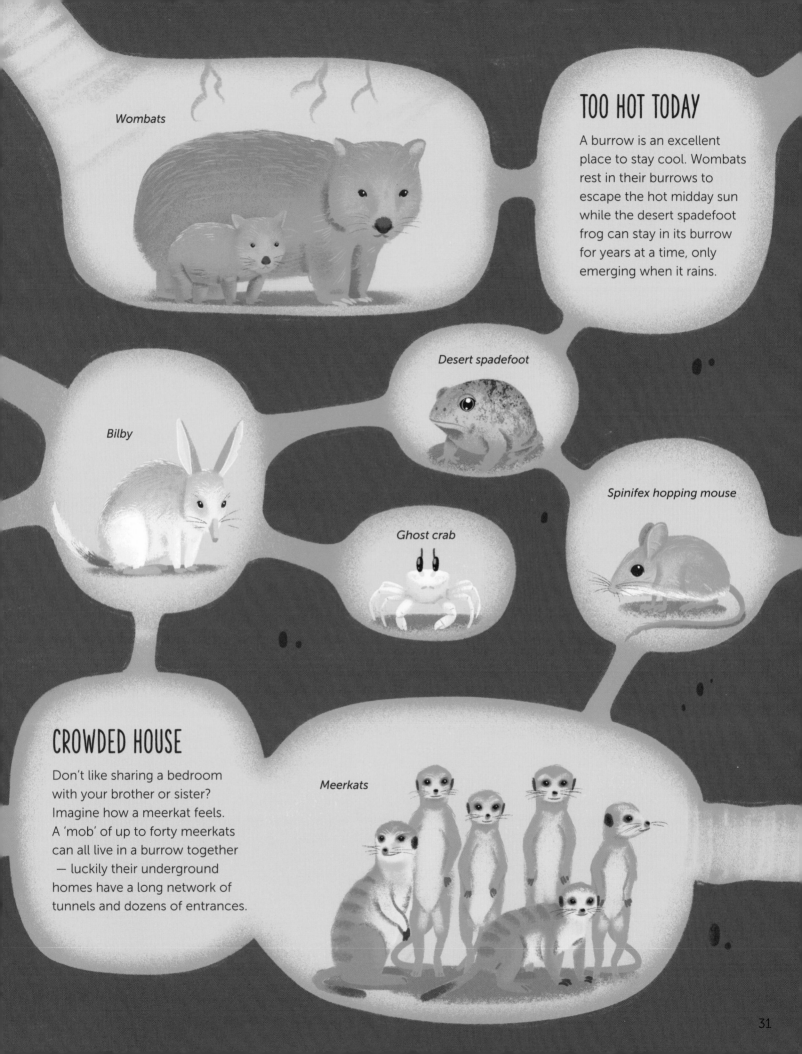

Wombats

TOO HOT TODAY

A burrow is an excellent place to stay cool. Wombats rest in their burrows to escape the hot midday sun while the desert spadefoot frog can stay in its burrow for years at a time, only emerging when it rains.

Desert spadefoot

Bilby

Ghost crab

Spinifex hopping mouse

CROWDED HOUSE

Don't like sharing a bedroom with your brother or sister? Imagine how a meerkat feels. A 'mob' of up to forty meerkats can all live in a burrow together — luckily their underground homes have a long network of tunnels and dozens of entrances.

Meerkats

THE CITY BELOW

What lies beneath your feet?
If you live in a city, it's a maze of twisting tunnels, secret vaults and a lot of pipes. We use underground networks to transport people, electricity, water and waste across vast distances.

If you catch the tube or see construction workers fixing a broken pipe you might get a glimpse into a world that mostly remains hidden.

PIPE DOWN

It's easy to forget that when you flick on a light switch or turn on a tap the energy and water you're about to use has travelled hundreds of kilometres underground to get to you. Pipes and cables are knitted beneath our cities, but we only notice them when something goes wrong.

SECRET STATIONS

As cities change, so do the tube tunnels beneath them. If a station doesn't suit modern trains or doesn't fit enough people it might be left abandoned. There's even a hidden railway under London that was used just to transport the post!

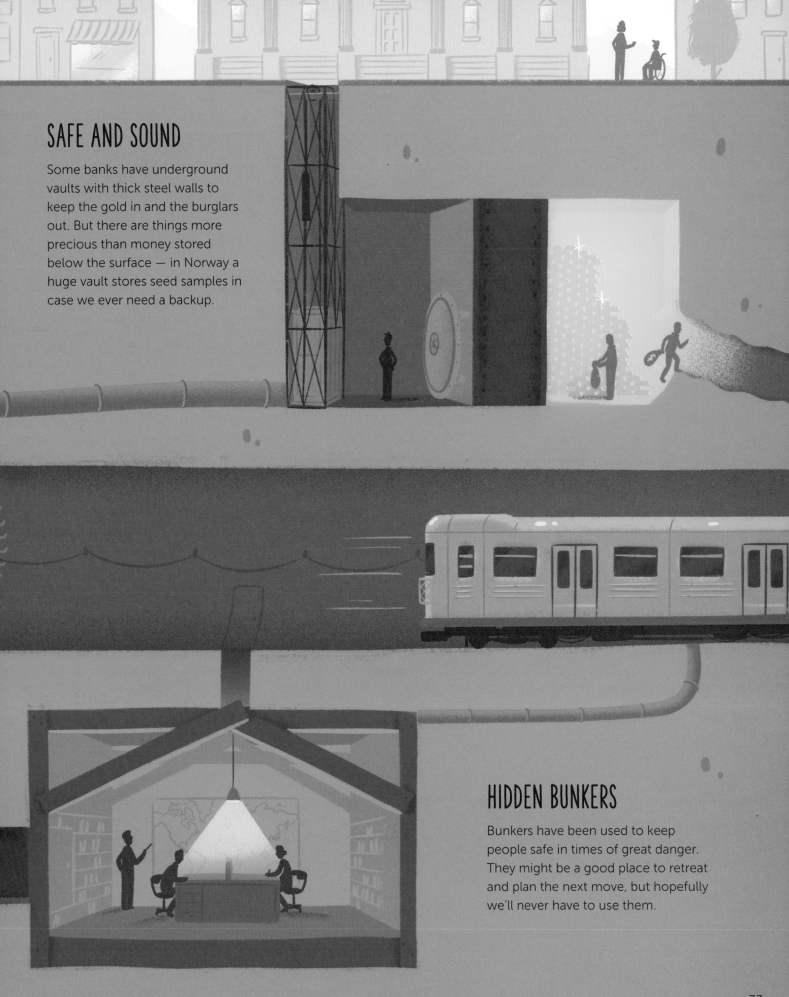

SAFE AND SOUND

Some banks have underground vaults with thick steel walls to keep the gold in and the burglars out. But there are things more precious than money stored below the surface — in Norway a huge vault stores seed samples in case we ever need a backup.

HIDDEN BUNKERS

Bunkers have been used to keep people safe in times of great danger. They might be a good place to retreat and plan the next move, but hopefully we'll never have to use them.

IN THE SEWERS

Can you smell something? We've reached the sewers, the final journey for everything we flush. Sewers are a vital part of any modern city, and while they might seem a bit gross just imagine life without them. In centuries past, waste ran through the street or was just thrown out a window.

Spare a thought for those who work down here too. Not only do they have to keep everything flowing smoothly, but they have to do it while avoiding the rats (and maybe alligators too).

SEWER TOUR

Sewer sightseeing was a popular pastime in 19th century Paris. Tourists dressed in their best clothes would hop on boats to be navigated through the underworld. Mind where you step!

LOST AND FOUND

Dinosaur fossils, precious rings and lost treasure have all been found in the sewers. There's even a legend that tells of an alligator prowling the New York sewer system!

DIGGING DEEPER

Giant boring machines help our cities grow deeper all the time. Who knows what else we might find down there?

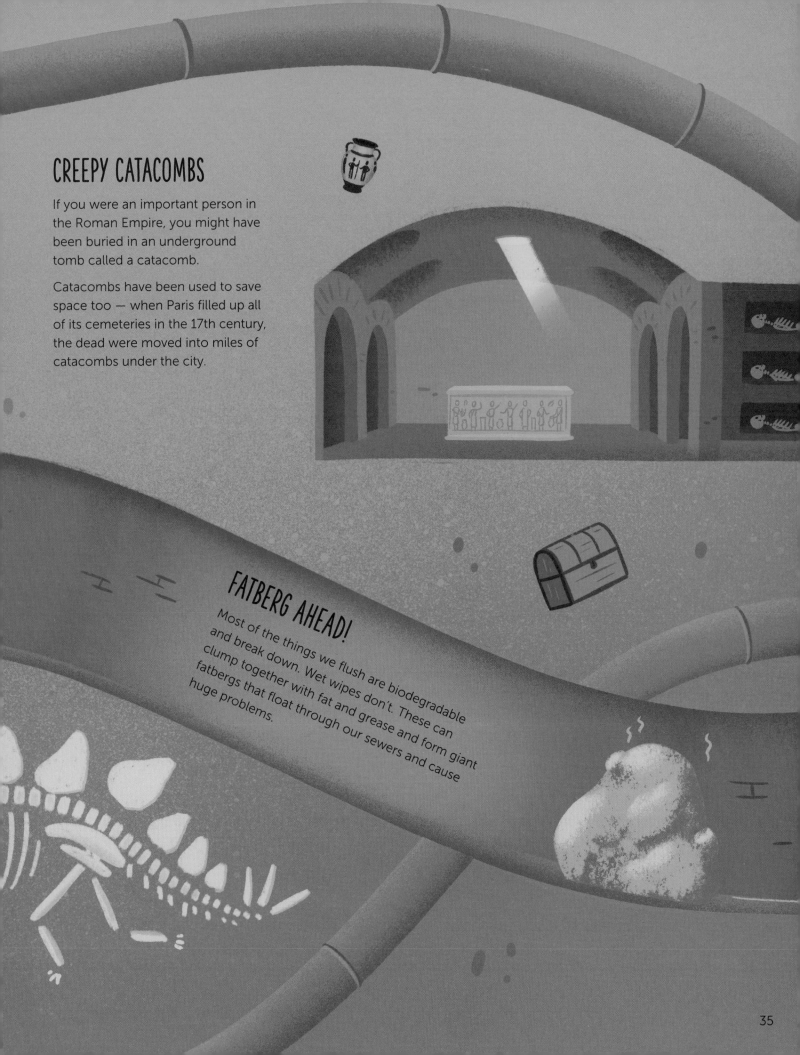

CREEPY CATACOMBS

If you were an important person in the Roman Empire, you might have been buried in an underground tomb called a catacomb.

Catacombs have been used to save space too — when Paris filled up all of its cemeteries in the 17th century, the dead were moved into miles of catacombs under the city.

FATBERG AHEAD!

Most of the things we flush are biodegradable and break down. Wet wipes don't. These can clump together with fat and grease and form giant fatbergs that float through our sewers and cause huge problems.

BURIED SECRETS

Much of what we know about the past comes from what we dig up. Kings and queens were honoured with gold and jewels, but coins and games often tell better stories about how everyday people lived. How different was it to the way that we live now?

Sutton Hoo helmet

Terracotta warrior

LIFE AND DEATH

In some cultures, objects to help in the afterlife were buried with people that died. Ornate armour, Viking longships and even an army of terracotta warriors were left with kings and emperors for their journey onward.

Oseberg Viking ship

Eagle fibula brooch

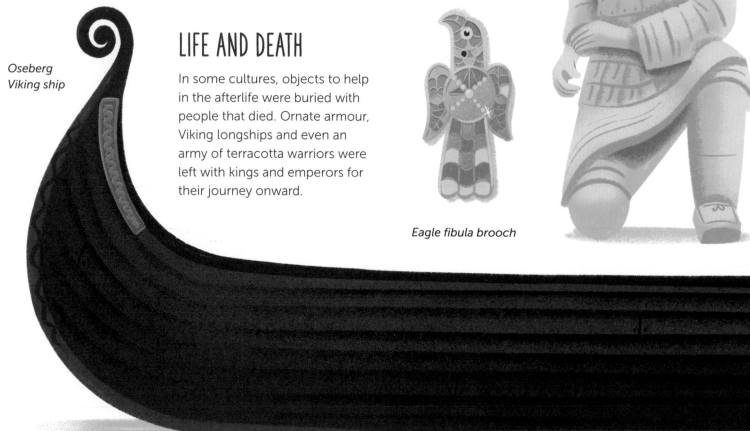

Lewis chessmen

WRITTEN IN STONE

Objects can hold clues to entire civilisations. A buried coin might tell us who was king, a stone tablet could decipher a lost language and a bronze disc can show us how people studied the stars long ago.

Mesopotamian clay tablet

Rosetta Stone

Nebra sky disk

Ancient coins

Egyptian coffin

FINDERS KEEPERS?

Who does the past belong to? It's a question that wasn't often asked when objects were taken from the ground. Some now sit in museums, where everyone can learn from them, but others belong with the descendents of those who left them behind.

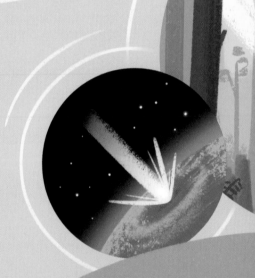

2. LIFE TAKES OFF...

Paleozoic Era
541–252 million years ago

As continents shifted around, life got more complicated beneath the waves. Worm-like organisms evolved to eat bacteria in the oceans, followed by the appearance of arthropods such as trilobites. Ferns and trees started to pop up while fish evolved and decided to give dry land a go.

1. A HOT START

Precambrian
4.6 billion years ago

Earth wasn't much fun for its first few billion years. It began as a fiery place, the molten-hot surface prone to volcanic eruptions and asteroid impacts. Things slowly began to cool as water vapour in the atmosphere fell as rain, creating the first oceans. Luckily bacteria was among the mix, seeding the very first signs of life.

3. ...WITH A FEW BUMPS

Permian–Triassic extinction event
252 million years ago

Just when the party gets going, an extinction event comes along. The Paleozoic era finished with a mass extinction that ended almost all life on Earth. We're not exactly sure how, but it may have been a large asteroid.

5. MEET THE MAMMALS

Cenozoic Era
66 million years ago until present day

Without dinosaurs it was the mammals' turn to take the spotlight. Pieces of Pangea rearranged into our continents as new species evolved — the ancestors of many animals we know today.

DEEP TIME

You can think about time a bit like a river. Sometimes things on Earth move slowly and at other times the world has undergone rapid change. There have been some big ripples but so far life has found a way to keep flowing.

4. REPTILES RULE

Mesozoic Era
252–66 million years ago

It took almost 10 million years for life to bounce back. When it did, reptiles dominated the sky, land and sea, as pterosaurs, dinosaurs and marine reptiles. The supercontinent Pangea slowly broke apart, but like the Paleozoic Era, this one ended with a bang.

6. HUMANS ARRIVE

Anthropocene

As humans we have barely dipped a toe into the river of time, yet our ripples are huge. We've changed our planet so much that some scientists have named an epoch after us — the Anthropocene. How long will our time last?

CLUES TO THE PAST

Millions of years ago, a dinosaur died. Its body fell into a river where its skeleton was covered in silt and mud. Over thousands of years, this hardened while its bones began to dissolve — replaced by minerals that then turned to rock. It had become a fossil. Ancient plants, shells and insects have been found preserved in rock, ice and amber and can show us what the world looked like long ago.

Brittle star fossil

Ammonite fossil

Trilobite fossil

FROZEN IN TIME

Seed fern fossil

Finding a fossil can tell us a lot. A fossilised fern in the desert might have once come from a lush forest. A seashell on a mountain tells us vast continents were once underwater. Fossils can even show us what the future might look like in a rapidly warming world.

Tyrannosaurus rex fossil

WHAT WAS FOR LUNCH?

Not every fossil can be a glamorous skeleton. Fossilised poo is called coprolite. Far from being gross, these trace fossils hold a wealth of information about what (or who) their creator ate for breakfast.

Coprolite

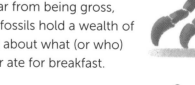

Fossil footprint

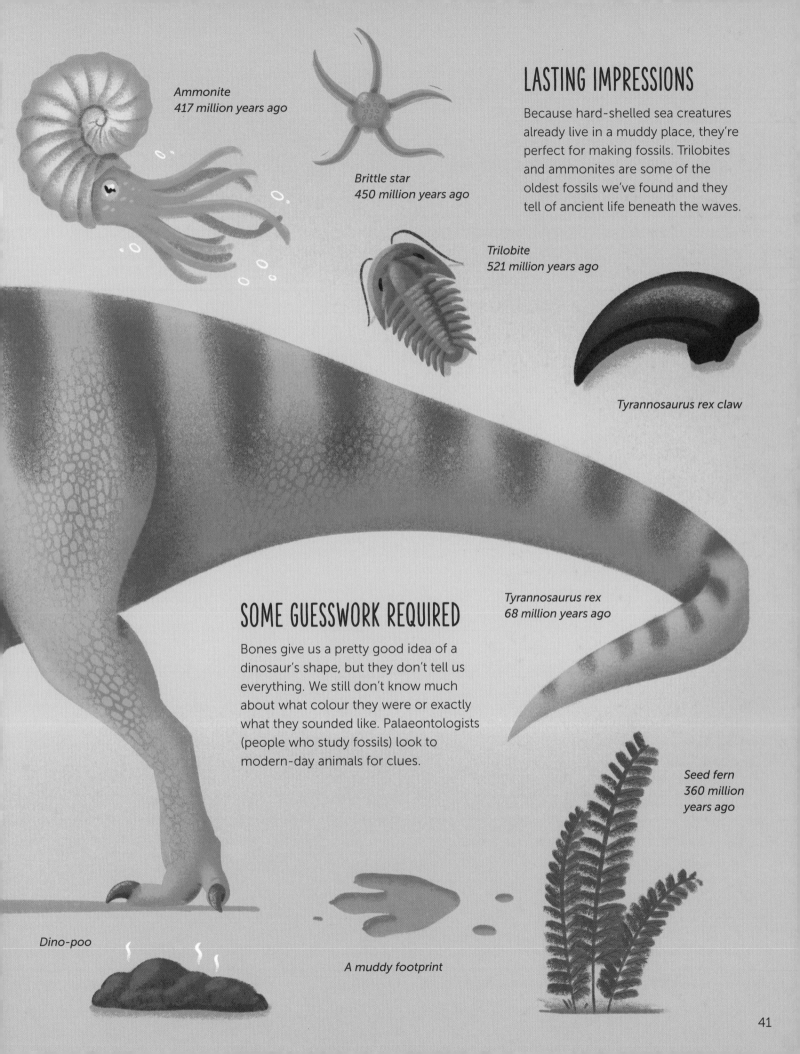

Ammonite
417 million years ago

Brittle star
450 million years ago

LASTING IMPRESSIONS

Because hard-shelled sea creatures already live in a muddy place, they're perfect for making fossils. Trilobites and ammonites are some of the oldest fossils we've found and they tell of ancient life beneath the waves.

Trilobite
521 million years ago

Tyrannosaurus rex claw

SOME GUESSWORK REQUIRED

Tyrannosaurus rex
68 million years ago

Bones give us a pretty good idea of a dinosaur's shape, but they don't tell us everything. We still don't know much about what colour they were or exactly what they sounded like. Palaeontologists (people who study fossils) look to modern-day animals for clues.

Seed fern
360 million years ago

Dino-poo

A muddy footprint

WHAT WE LEAVE BEHIND

The layers of rock we're standing on took billions of years to form. The layer of rubbish took no time at all. Our love of fast fashion and the latest gadgets has left us with a lot of waste we'd rather forget, but the things we bury have a way of coming back to the surface.

OUT OF FASHION

Everyone loves a bargain, but at what cost? Cheap fabrics like nylon take decades to break down, while polyester can take centuries. Our planet is beautiful enough without needing to wear our old clothes.

Nylon
40+ years to break down

Rubber
50+ years

E-WASTE

Our wave of new technology has left a huge pile of rubbish in its wake. If electronic waste isn't properly recycled it can leak toxic chemicals into our soil, air and water. It's poisonous to the land and animals (which includes us too).

Electronic waste
Up to 1,000,000 years to break down

FOOD FOR THOUGHT

Did you know that a third of the food we produce ends up in the bin? Organic waste makes up a huge chunk of landfill, and when it rots it releases greenhouse gases that contribute to climate change.

Organic waste
1-6 months to break down

Aluminum can
100+ years to break down

Battery
100+ years to break down

Plastic bag
20+ years to break down

THE PLASTIC PROBLEM

Plastic is cheap to make, it doesn't shatter and it lasts a long time — all qualities that make it terrible for the planet. Plastic can take hundreds of years to decompose, releasing harmful chemicals and choking wildlife along the way.

Plastic toothbrush
500+ years to break down

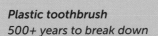

Plastic bottle
450+ years to break down

OUT OF SIGHT, OUT OF MIND

We've buried some seriously nasty stuff under our home. Radioactive waste, a byproduct of nuclear power, can stay dangerous for millions of years and we are yet to find a good way to store it.

THE PATH AHEAD

It's easy to think about time as something that's already happened, but it can be harder to imagine it stretching out far ahead. What will the world look like to your great-great-grandchildren? Will they still get to meet the animals and visit the places in this book?

If we are going to leave a healthy planet for future generations, one thing's for certain — we need to make deep changes. Some of the brightest minds are working on it right now, and you might even be one of them.

YOU ARE HERE

Earth is the third planet from the
Sun, and the fifth biggest in our solar
system. It takes us a little under 24
hours to spin on Earth's axis, and a
little over 365 days to orbit the Sun.

THINK LOCAL

It's easy to feel lonely in the universe, but just remember how many neighbours we've got. Andromeda is the nearest major galaxy to our Milky Way, just 2.5 million light-years away. That's a long way to go for a cup of sugar.

DEEP SPACE

Right now you're sitting on a small rock spinning around a burning star. There's seven other planets doing the same thing, along with hundreds of moons and millions of asteroids and comets. All of that sits in the arm of the Milky Way Galaxy, which is orbiting a supermassive black hole. Feeling dizzy yet?

THE KUIPER BELT

If you're going to leave our solar system and venture into deep space, you'll need to pass through the Kuiper belt. We think this icy ring is made up of our solar system's leftover bits, and it's where you'll find dwarf planets such as Pluto.

WHAT WE CAN SEE

Look up at the night sky. What can you see? If you're lucky, it might be one of the eight planets in our solar system. Beyond that you might see some of the hundreds of millions of stars in our galaxy, or one of the billions of galaxies in our universe. Or it might be a cloudy night.

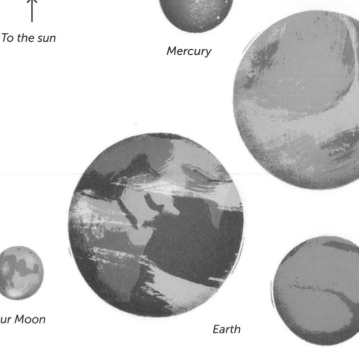

↑
To the sun

Mercury

Venus

Our Moon

Earth

Mars

LIFE SOUP

The soup of life has a very complicated recipe. Take a planet and make sure it orbits a sun at just the right distance (not too hot, not too cold). Add oxygen, carbon, hydrogen, nitrogen and a sprinkling of other elements in just the right amount. Wait several billion years and cross your fingers.

Jupiter

Saturn

PUT A RING ON IT

It takes all planets to make a universe. Some, like Venus, have a baking hot surface covered in volcanoes. Others, like Jupiter, are mostly made of gas and have no real surface at all. Some wear rings of ice and rock like Saturn, and some have dozens of moons caught in their orbit, like Uranus.

Uranus

Neptune

GALAXIES

Galaxies are made up of dust, gas and billions of stars all held together by gravity and dark matter. Some form as spirals, some as ellipses (ovals), and some as blobby irregular shapes. Our solar system sits on the arm of a barred spiral galaxy, the Milky Way.

Spiral galaxy

Elliptical galaxy

Irregular galaxy

Nebula

THE BIRTH OF A STAR

Stars are born and stars die, just like us. A nebula is a huge cloud of dust and gas, sometimes formed from the explosion of a dying star. Over hundreds of thousands of years gravity can clump these bits together until they begin to collapse under their own weight, heating up and giving birth to a new protostar.

BLACK HOLES

If a dying star collapses on itself, its matter can get squished into a very small space. This can create a black hole, with so much gravity that stars, planets and even light can't escape the pull. Without that light we can't see what's inside.

WHAT WE CAN'T SEE

Most of the universe is made up of stuff we can't see. Luckily the things we can see give us clues to what we can't. If an apple falls from a tree, there must be an invisible force pulling it down. If deep in the universe stars keep disappearing, there could be a hole somewhere nearby.

GRAVITY

Without gravity, you and this book would float to the ceiling. Gravity is an invisible force which pulls objects together. The more mass an object has, the more gravity. Gravity keeps the moon orbiting our planet, and our planet orbiting the Sun.

DARK MATTER

Matter is the teeny tiny stuff that makes up everything you can see. Dark matter is the teeny tiny stuff that makes up things you can't see. Finding dark matter is a bit like looking for a missing sock — we know it has to be there somewhere, we just can't see it directly.

INTO THE UNKNOWN

If you have ever looked up at the Moon and wondered what it would be like to visit, you might soon get your chance. We've been launching spacecraft to explore our solar system for more than half a century and with every success (and failure) we learn more about the amazing universe we live in.

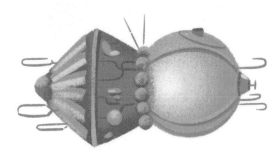

Vostok
1960–1963

SMALL STEPS

The Russian *Sputnik 1* was the first spacecraft to successfully orbit the Earth. This sparked an intense competition between nations to launch humans and probes into space, and later set foot on the Moon.

Apollo
1961–1972

Gemini
1964–1966

Soyuz
1966–present

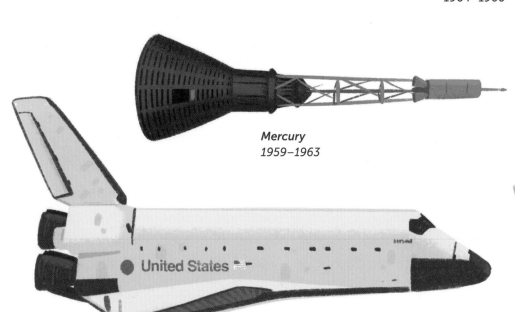

Mercury
1959–1963

Orion
2014–present

Space Shuttle
1981–2011

DEEP SPACE

When it comes to travelling in deep space, humans haven't got very far — but we're working on it. The *Orion* spacecraft is designed to support human life in deep space, with the hope of taking us to Mars and beyond.

Shenzhou
1999–present

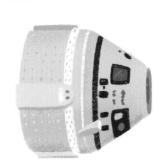

Starliner
2019–present

PROBING AROUND

For the places we can't get to yet, probes can go for us. They come in all shapes and sizes but share the same goal — to collect information and send it back to Earth. Some are designed to study the Sun, orbit other planets or even land on asteroids!

Sakigake
Flyby of Halley's Comet

Pioneer 6
Studied solar wind

New Horizons
Flyby of Pluto

Pioneer 10
Flyby of Jupiter

Juno
Orbiting Jupiter

Mariner 10
Flyby of Mercury and Venus

Galileo
Orbited Jupiter

STILL TRAVELLING ON

Voyager 1 and its twin *Voyager 2* have travelled the furthest from Earth. Launched in 1977, *Voyager 1* flew by Jupiter and Saturn — and then it kept going. And going. It's now made it past our solar system, through the Kuiper belt and into interstellar space. Talk about a long trip!

Rosetta
Orbited a comet

Cassini
Visited Saturn

Voyager 1
Now in Interstellar space

OSIRIS-REx
Gathering samples from an asteroid

53

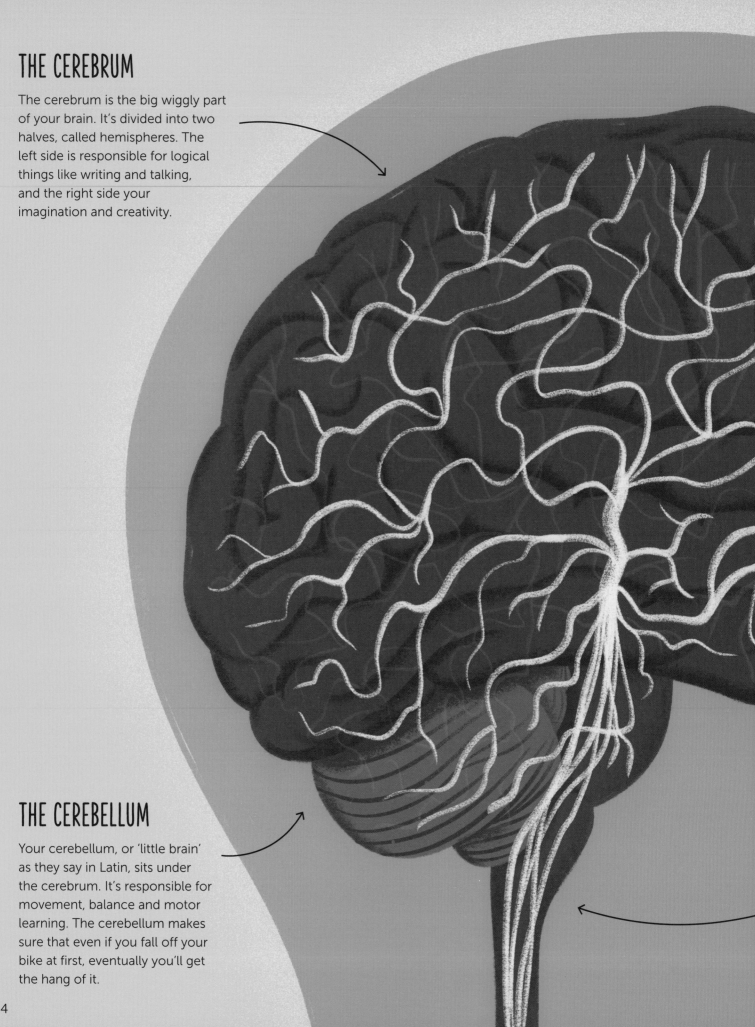

THE CEREBRUM

The cerebrum is the big wiggly part of your brain. It's divided into two halves, called hemispheres. The left side is responsible for logical things like writing and talking, and the right side your imagination and creativity.

THE CEREBELLUM

Your cerebellum, or 'little brain' as they say in Latin, sits under the cerebrum. It's responsible for movement, balance and motor learning. The cerebellum makes sure that even if you fall off your bike at first, eventually you'll get the hang of it.

ELECTRIC HIGHWAY

Your brain works a bit like a relay race. The runners are cells called neurons, passing messages to each other at electric speed. Billions of neurons transmit messages between your brain and nervous system, telling your body what to do.

DEEP INSIDE

You don't need to go to the bottom of the ocean or deep underground to find a complex web of wires and a host of weird creatures — look no further than your own body. Every nerve, muscle and bone has a different job to do, and most of the time you don't even notice them doing it.

THE STEM

The brainstem connects the cerebrum and cerebellum to the spinal cord. It's in charge of some pretty important jobs like breathing, digesting and keeping your heart pumping.

SWEET DREAMS

Just because you slow down at night, it doesn't mean that your mind does. While you sleep your brain is busy storing memories, solving creative problems and clearing out toxins — ready for a brand new day.

THE SKIN YOU'RE IN

The largest organ in your body isn't your brain or lungs, it's your skin. This amazing wetsuit protects you from extreme temperatures, unfriendly chemicals and germs. It's also packed with nerves, glands and follicles that allow you to touch, sweat and grow hair.

UNDER YOUR SKIN

Your body is made up of squishy bits (organs) that are protected by hard bits (a skeleton). It's intertwined with a network of nerves and blood vessels all wrapped up in muscles and skin. Every body is different but they can all do amazing things.

SHOW OFF YOUR MUSCLES

Muscles are good at two things: contracting and relaxing. When they contract, they can pull bones and blood vessels that allow you to dance, sing or run a marathon (or sit back and read a book). Muscles can't push, so they often come in pairs to pull from each direction.

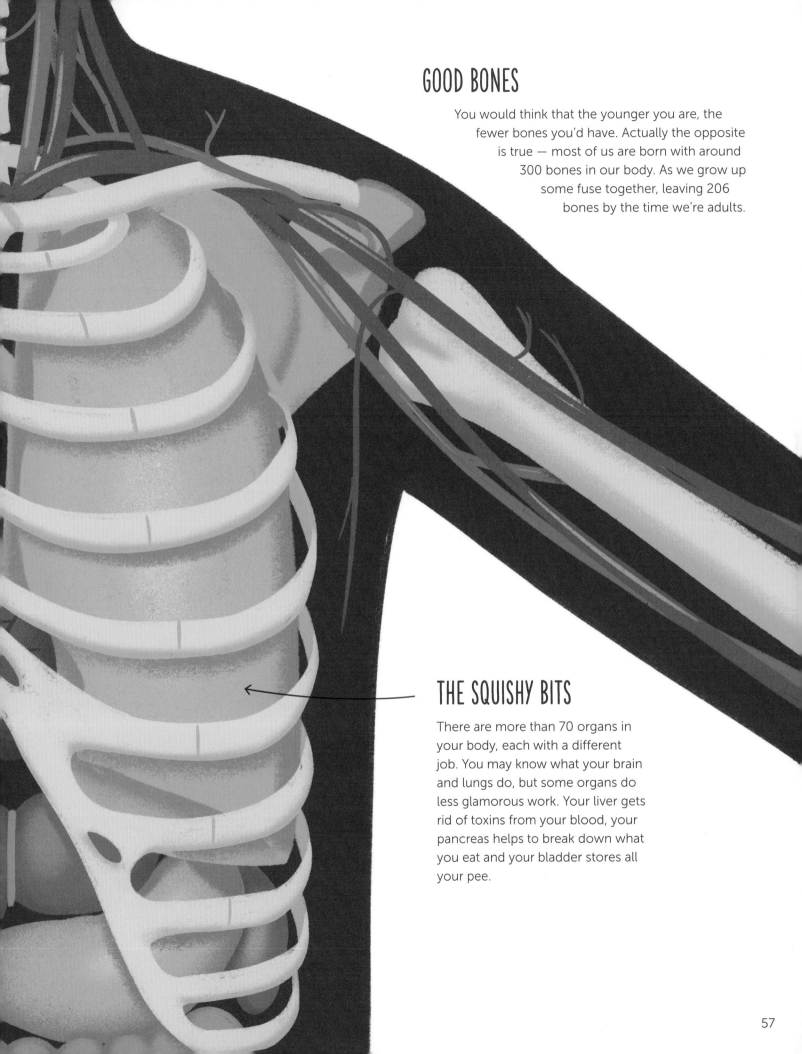

GOOD BONES

You would think that the younger you are, the
fewer bones you'd have. Actually the opposite
is true — most of us are born with around
300 bones in our body. As we grow up
some fuse together, leaving 206
bones by the time we're adults.

THE SQUISHY BITS

There are more than 70 organs in
your body, each with a different
job. You may know what your brain
and lungs do, but some organs do
less glamorous work. Your liver gets
rid of toxins from your blood, your
pancreas helps to break down what
you eat and your bladder stores all
your pee.

A TEAM OF TRILLIONS

Your body is home to trillions of tiny workers. Some are very busy with lots of important things to do, others are just enjoying the free food in your gut. There are a few bad guys around but don't worry, security is already on to it.

Muscle cells

Red blood cells

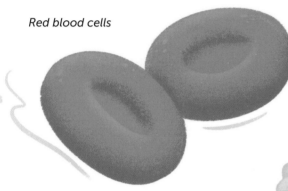

*Sex cells
Egg and Sperm*

Skin cells

White blood cell

A JOB TO DO

All living things are made up of one or more cells, and we've got trillions. Some, like blood cells, fight infection and carry oxygen around the body. Others can grow skin, mend bone or even change into other cells.

Fat cell

Nerve cell

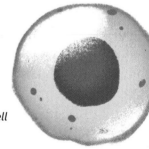

Stem cell

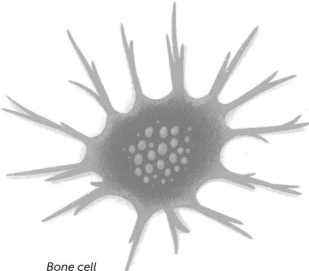

Bone cell

CELL-MAIL

Cells talk to one another by passing chemical signals. They can do this in different ways, such as directly bumping into each other or by releasing them into the bloodstream.

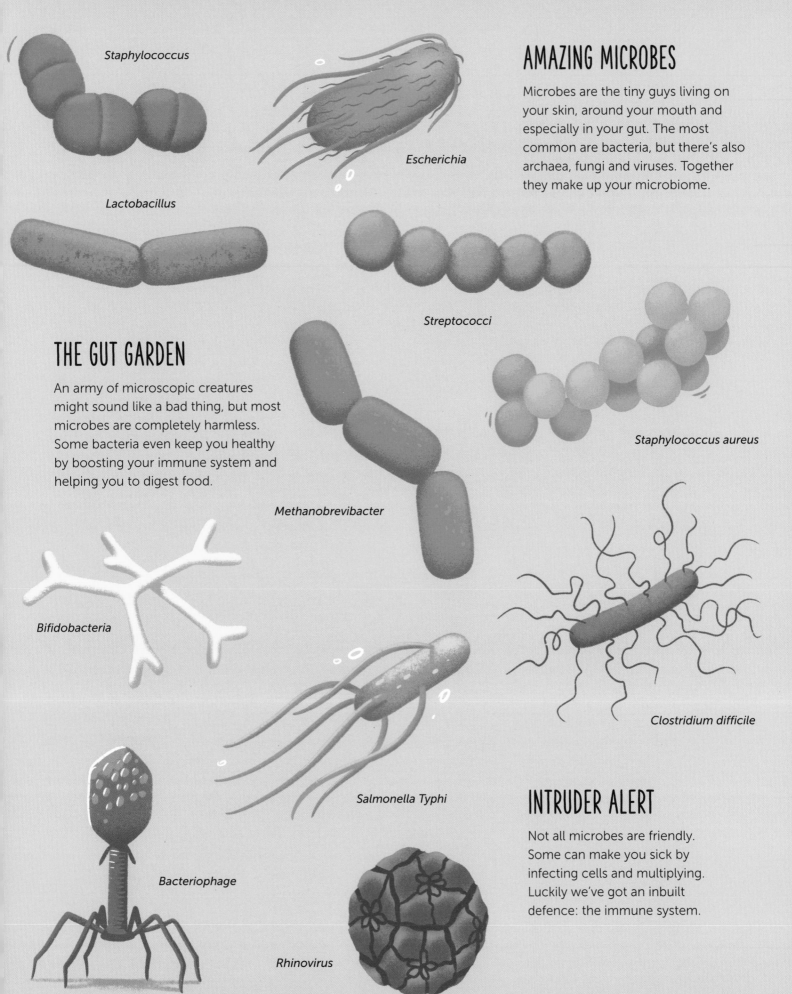

Staphylococcus

Escherichia

Lactobacillus

AMAZING MICROBES

Microbes are the tiny guys living on your skin, around your mouth and especially in your gut. The most common are bacteria, but there's also archaea, fungi and viruses. Together they make up your microbiome.

Streptococci

THE GUT GARDEN

An army of microscopic creatures might sound like a bad thing, but most microbes are completely harmless. Some bacteria even keep you healthy by boosting your immune system and helping you to digest food.

Staphylococcus aureus

Methanobrevibacter

Bifidobacteria

Clostridium difficile

Salmonella Typhi

INTRUDER ALERT

Not all microbes are friendly. Some can make you sick by infecting cells and multiplying. Luckily we've got an inbuilt defence: the immune system.

Bacteriophage

Rhinovirus

DEEP CONNECTIONS

Even though they're millions of miles apart, the distant corners of the deep still have things in common. Finding deep connections can help us understand our universe and how we fit into it.

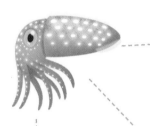

NASA studies deep-sea vents to find out what life on other planets could look like.

Scientists look to deep-sea creatures to learn more about how our own minds work.

There are more microbes in your body than there are stars in the Milky Way.

The neural network in our brains looks a lot like a map of the universe.

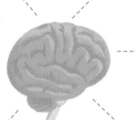

The microbes living in your gut can affect your mood.

Some fungi in the Amazon rainforest use bioluminescence, just like deep-sea creatures.

Scientists think trees can communicate using chemical signals – the same way our brains work.

What fossils will we leave behind?

Scientists have found microbes that have been alive since the time of the dinosaurs.

Fungi survived the same extinction event that killed the dinosaurs.

SURVIVING THE DEEP

The deep can be a dangerous place. Here's a few handy
tips to survive and thrive from those who know it best.

MAKE LIGHT

Scared of the dark? Not to worry,
make your own! Bioluminescence
is the process some organisms
use to create their own light.
It's a very handy skill to disguise
your shape or to lure in lunch.

GROW ARMOUR

If you've got soft skin, grow some
armour. Having your bones on the
outside is called an exoskeleton,
and it's a good way to protect
your squishy inside. You will need
to shed it every so often; it won't
grow with you.

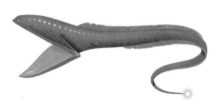

EAT WHEN YOU CAN

Food is scarce in the deep, so
when a meal comes along, make
sure your mouth is big enough
to fit it all in. If you do manage to
find breakfast, sit back and take a
break — it's going to take a long
time to digest.

BLEND IN...

How long can you stay still and
pretend to be a stick? If it's for
a while, you might be able to
master the art of camouflage.
It's a great way to avoid getting
eaten, or to sneak up on someone
who's about to be.

...OR STAND OUT

Sometimes it's better to stand out
from the crowd. If you're looking
to find a mate or warn an enemy
that you're not to be messed
with, being bright and colourful
might be the way to go.

ADAPT

The most important survival
skill isn't brawn or brains —
it's adapting to change. Evolving
to suit your environment is the
best way to flourish in the deep.
Can we adapt to thrive in our
changing world?

GLOSSARY

Bacteria small organisms (living things), that are made up of a single cell. They can be found in all natural environments.

Civilisation developed society of people living together in communities, often with a shared way of life, culture and beliefs. The ancient Romans, Egyptians, and Aztecs are all examples of civilisations from ancient times.

Colony group of organisms from the same species that live together and interact closely with each other

Crustacean animal with a hard shell (called an exoskeleton) and several pairs of legs, which usually lives in water. Shrimps, lobsters and crabs are crustaceans.

Decipher work out the meaning of something that is difficult to read or understand

Decomposition process of something dead, such as an animal or plant, breaking down (rotting) into simpler matter, such as carbon dioxide, water, and nutrients

Evolve gradual change of a living thing over many, many generations. All living things that are alive today evolved from earlier types.

Extinction dying out of an entire species, so that there are no more of that animal, plant, or other organism left on Earth

Fungus (plural: fungi) simple organism (living thing) that is not an animal or plant. Types of fungi include mushrooms, truffles, moulds, mildews and yeasts.

Larva (plural: larvae) life stage of an insect once it has hatched from an egg, before it changes into its adult form. A caterpillar is a butterfly larva.

Mass amount of matter an object contains. It is measured in grams and kilograms.

Microbiome community of microorganisms (such as bacteria, viruses and fungi) that live together in a particular environment and especially the collection of microorganisms living in or on the human body

Nuclear power use of nuclear reactions to release energy, which is converted into electricity

Organism individual animal, plant, or single-celled life form

Predator animal that hunts, kills and eats other animals for food

Prey animal that is hunted and eaten by a predator

Scavenger animal that eats the remains of other animals that have already died

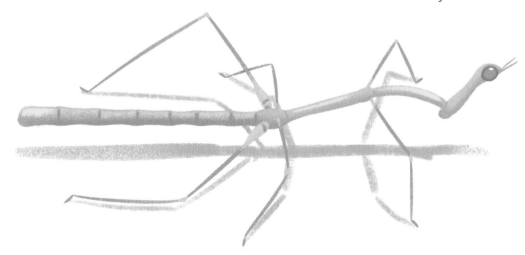

INDEX

A

adaptation 8, 10, 12, 29, 61
Amazon rainforest 17, 18, 60
Anthropocene epoch 39
ants 20–21, 22
arthropods 11, 38

B

bacteria 10, 38, 59
badgers 30
beetles 23
bioluminescence 12, 60, 61
birds 17, 18, 19, 30
black holes 47, 50
body, human 54–59
bones 40, 57
brain, human 54–55, 60
bunkers 33
buried objects 36–37
burrows 30–31

C

camouflage 23, 61
canopy, forest 17
catacombs 35
caves 28–29
cells 58
centipedes 23
climate change 43
coprolites 40
crabs 11, 31

DE

dark matter 49, 50
dinosaurs 39, 40–41
dreaming 55

e-waste 42
Earth's layers 24–25
Earth's timeline 38–39
evolution 38–39
exoskeletons 11, 61
extinction events 38, 60

F

fast fashion 42
fatbergs 35
first life on Earth 38
fish 10, 12, 13, 17, 29, 38
food waste 43
forests 16–23
fossils 40–41, 60
frogs 18, 31
fungi 16, 22, 59, 60

GH

galaxies 47, 48, 49
gigantism 10–11
glowworms 29
gravity 49, 50

hydrothermal vents 9, 10

IJ

immune system 59
insects 19, 20–21, 22, 23
invertebrates 12
isopods 10, 11

jungle 18–21

KLMN

Kraken 10
Kuiper belt 47, 53

Mariana Trench 15
meerkats 31
microbes 59, 60
Milky Way 47, 49, 60
minerals 9, 26–27, 28, 40
mining 27
monkeys 17, 18, 19
muscles 56, 58

OPQ

ocean floor 9, 14–15
ocean trenches 9, 14, 15
ocean zones 8–9
oceans 8–15, 38, 60
organs 56, 57

Pangea 38
peccaries 16
planets 46, 47, 48
plastic waste 15, 43
predators 8, 19

RS

radioactive waste 43
rocks 24, 26, 42

scavengers 13
sewers 34–35
shipwrecks 14–15
skin 56, 58
solar system 46–49, 52, 53
space 46–51
space probes 53
spacecraft 52–53
squid 10, 11, 12
stalagmites and stalactites 28, 29
stars 37, 48, 49, 50
submersibles 14
subways 32

TUVW

trees 16, 17, 38, 60
troglobites 29
tube worms 9, 10

underground 28–35
understory 16
universe 46–51

vaults 33
volcanoes 14, 25, 38, 48
Voyager spacecraft 53

waste 21, 34, 42–43
whales 8
wombats 31

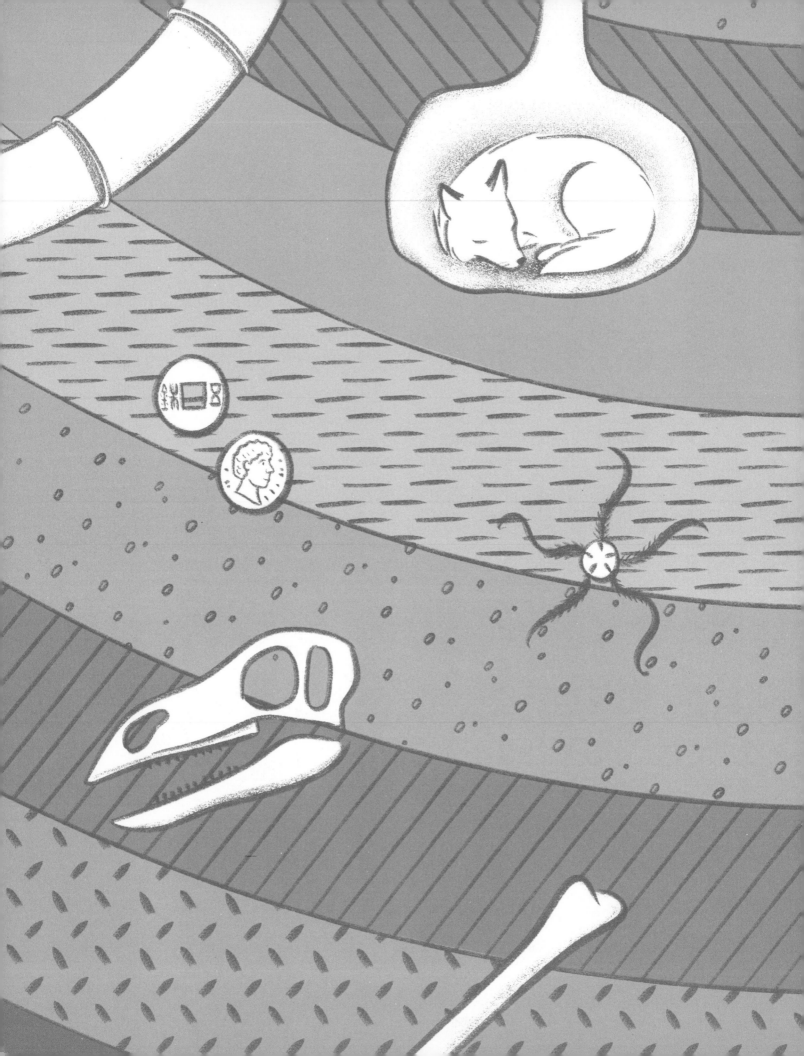